Blue Ridge Parkway

impressions

photography by Pat and Chuck Blackley

text by Cara Ellen Modisett

FARCOUNTRY
PRESS

RIGHT: The Blue Ridge Parkway curves around the shoulders of Mount Mitchell during a storm. At 6,684 feet, Mount Mitchell is the highest peak in the eastern U.S., towering in the ancient Black Mountains. North Carolina's Parkway winds along some of the tallest, most rugged ridges in the Appalachian chain.

TITLE PAGE: The ridges march away into the blue distance, framed by rhododendron and evergreens. This view is from near the Cowee Mountains overlook in North Carolina, in Cherokee country. Cowee was called Ka-wi by the Native Americans, roughly translated as "Place of the Deer Clan."

FRONT COVER: The names of Appalachian peaks and valleys echo the birds and beasts that live on them. Ravens Roost, at Virginia milepost 10.7, is pictured here just beyond a thicket of pink-blooming azaleas. The rock outcropping serves as a perch for soaring blackbirds as well as for hang gliders and rock climbers.

BACK COVER: Shadows lace the ground in autumn where the road passes through Humpback Rocks area at the Parkway's northern end in Virginia. The Appalachian Trail, another north-south route that follows and crisscrosses the Parkway along its 469 miles, runs through here, as did the Old Howardsville Turnpike, a mid-nineteenth-century trade route.

ISBN: 1-56037-252-4
Photography © Pat & Chuck Blackley
Text © Cara Ellen Modisett
© 2003 Farcountry Press

Foreword

**by FRIENDS of the
Blue Ridge Parkway, Inc.**

The Blue Ridge Parkway is a special thing—a 469-mile road that climbs the ridge lines and peaks of the Appalachian Mountains, every year carrying 23.5 million visitors between Shenandoah National Park and the Great Smoky Mountains.

It's one of the most loved parks in the country, and for that very reason Dr. Harley Jolley has termed it an endangered species. Residential and commercial growth, pollution, and non-native predatory insects are taking their toll on the Parkway's views, trees, and wildlife.

It's not going unnoticed.

As of April 2003, the membership of the Roanoke, Virginia-based, nonprofit FRIENDS of the Blue Ridge Parkway, Inc., has topped 4,500.

These are 4,500 individuals who recognize the historic and natural value of the Blue Ridge Parkway—and the risk to its survival.

In partnership with the National Park Service as well as other organizations, businesses, and agencies, the staff and membership of FRIENDS have made it their mission to protect the Parkway and raise public awareness of this national treasure so that future generations will continue to experience its unique journey.

That experience can be a grand experience—469 miles of views that stretch for miles through the mists and clear skies of the East.

It can be an intimate experience—469 miles of moments; moments of peace, moments of learning, moments of rejuvenation, moments we are all seeking in a world irrevocably changed since September 11, 2001.

The Parkway is unusual among national parks in that it is linear, passing through two states (Virginia and North Carolina) and thirty-seven counties, touching human and natural communities along the way. The Parkway, called America's Most Scenic Drive, is within one day's drive of more than half of the population of the United States.

The Parkway is a rich tapestry, weaving natural beauty and history with human cultural heritage. It is America's living rural life museum, where basket-weavers, traditional Appalachian musicians, blacksmiths, and quilters bring the past to the present.

Historic sites such as gristmills, bridges, and one-room schoolhouses exist along the Parkway, and 350 miles of trails crisscross its length, connecting with the Appalachian Trail and even older pathways that wind through forests of hardwood, evergreen, and the endangered hemlock.

All special places of great beauty are affected by time, and the Blue Ridge Parkway is no exception. Residential and commercial development are compromising its views and wildlife habitats; pollution is fogging its clear air, and predators are destroying its trees.

Recognizing these threats, FRIENDS has pledged to help preserve, protect, and promote the outstanding natural beauty, ecological vitality, and cultural distinctiveness of the Blue Ridge Parkway and its surrounding scenic landscape, preserving this national treasure for future generations.

Founded in 1989 by the Blue Ridge Parkway superintendent, FRIENDS was organized as a nonprofit, membership-based organization to provide a link between Parkway visitors and the Parkway experience. It was believed that the organization and its members could be a catalyst for ensuring the preservation, conservation, and enhancement of the Parkway, which is not only a scenic asset but an economic one, bringing millions of visitors and tourists to Virginia and North Carolina every year.

A growing membership base reflects FRIENDS' vitality and grass-roots success. Many of the organization's key projects enlist the labor and energy, as well as the financial support, of members to accomplish its goals.

Here are our key projects:

•**Viewshed Protection**. Both FRIENDS and the Park Service feel that the Parkway's greatest threat today is encroaching development that impacts the visual experience. In 2003, Scenic America designated a 28-mile section of the Parkway near Roanoke, Virginia, as a Last Chance Landscape—and that phrase can be loosely applied to all 469 miles as communities expand and industry grows and natural, pristine places grow smaller and rarer.

The work of FRIENDS includes raising money, soliciting donations, and involving community volunteers in planting trees along the Parkway to buffer undesirable views. These viewsheds are landscaped to rebuild visitors' visual experiences along the Parkway, to reestablish wildlife habitats along the Parkway corridor, and to rebuild an ecological buffer against development.

•**The Volunteer in the Parks (VIP) Program** is a vital part of the National Park System. In 2002, 125,000 VIPs contributed 4.5 million hours at a value of more than $72 million dollars. At a cost of only $1.5 million, the return on the public's investment is astounding.

As corporate giving and federal funding decrease, National Park Service staff and resources become more limited. Volunteers play a critical role in filling the gaps by providing innumerable services, including assisting visitors in welcome centers, maintaining trails, staffing campgrounds, and providing historical interpretation and cultural demonstrations.

Volunteers' contributions to the experiences of Parkway visitors allow the Parkway to continue to educate contemporary travelers about the significance of the region's historical and cultural rural past.

The VIP Program administered by FRIENDS recruits and instructs volunteers from communities, universities, and businesses along the Parkway's corridor, and raises funds for volunteer programs and recognition events.

•**The Adopt-A-Trail Program** seeks to maintain the 350 miles of trails that adjoin the Parkway. FRIENDS recruits for and administers the Adopt-A-Trail Program for the National Park Service/Blue Ridge Parkway in a similar approach to the VIP program—asking people of all ages and walks of life to work together to build and maintain trails on Parkway land.

Community-based action is at the heart of FRIENDS' volunteer-based organization. Adopt-A-Trail and other projects like it empower community-based groups along the Blue Ridge Parkway corridor to collaborate in preserving a treasure in their own backyards.

FRIENDS is a vital and growing organization, working in partnership with the National Park Service and involving communities, individuals, other nonprofit organizations and businesses. Its members and supporters come from every state in the nation as well as from overseas.

In a time when life and the world are uncertain, when our view of the future is less than clear, the Blue Ridge Parkway stretches along mountains that are ageless, that have been here since long before we lived, that will be here for centuries to follow. Those mountains will remain healthy, beautiful, serene retreats from the busy world, as long as we continue to protect them from that same world.

For membership information or donations, contact:
FRIENDS of the Blue Ridge Parkway, Inc.
Post Office Box 20986
Roanoke, Virginia 24018
1-800-288-PARK (7275)
www.BlueRidgeFriends.org

Otter Creek flows 10 miles through forest to meet the James River. There have been unconfirmed sightings of mountain lions in this area. Camping and dining are both available here.

Roads have a mystery about them. Stand at the beginning, and the end is unseen. Beyond the first curve nothing is visible. A road is a journey in time, and like all journeys in time it is silent about its secrets, leaving them for the traveler to discover along the way.

The Blue Ridge Parkway, a unique road that climbs the ridges and dips into the valleys of the eastern Blue Ridge Mountains, spans 469 miles and 500 million years—a true journey in time. It's a road that is much older than its nearly seven decades, tracing a path through human, environmental and geologic history, stretching back centuries into millennia.

The Parkway's most immediate history has its roots in 1933, when President Franklin D. Roosevelt visited Shenandoah National Park's Civilian Conservation Corps (CCC) camps. In 1931, the CCC had begun construction under orders from President Herbert Hoover on Virginia's Skyline Drive, a scenic route that reaches from Front Royal to Afton. Roosevelt, the story goes, was inspired to encourage the creation of a similar road.

As is common in American society, politics, economics and legislation nearly overrode this vision. Politicians in the mountain states disagreed as to the route—one proposal suggested a route between Roanoke, Virginia and Greenville, South Carolina. Tennessee wanted to lay claim to some of the route. The federal government balked at funding a project that would only benefit a few states. State governments saw it as an economic boon; mountain residents saw it as an unwelcome intrusion.

North Carolina congressman Robert Lee Doughton introduced a bill in 1936. After barely passing in the House (the votes tallied up at 145 in favor of the Parkway, 131 against and 147 abstaining), the bill went through the Senate successfully. President Roosevelt's signature on June 22, 1936 made the Blue Ridge Parkway, or at least the plan for one, a reality.

America was deep in the Great Depression, and many people were unemployed. The country was establishing its state and national parks and forests, and men found work in the CCC, building cabins, blazing trails, laying down roads and landscaping. The Blue Ridge Parkway was a new and visionary project for an unemployed work force that included engineers, stonemasons and gardeners.

One young man stepped into the project and changed it forever.

Introduction

by Cara Ellen Modisett

Stanley Abbott, a landscape designer from New York, was hired to design this new linear park. Abbott's work extended beyond the line of the road and the planting of trees, however. He engendered the idea of what he called a necklace strung with pearls—visitor centers, campgrounds, lodges and trails all along the length of the Parkway—a recreational road through the mountains that would be one long destination in itself.

The final route for the Parkway created a link between two already-existing national parks, Shenandoah and Great Smoky Mountains. The Parkway would start at Afton Mountain, the southern terminus of Skyline Drive, and follow the ridgelines through Virginia and into North Carolina, ending 469 miles later at Cherokee (217 miles are in Virginia, 252 in North Carolina). Its elevation would vary between 668 feet (in Virginia's James River Valley, milepost 63.6) and 6,410 feet above sea level (North Carolina's Richland Balsam Knob, milepost 431.4).

Groundbreaking began on September 11, 1935 at Cumberland Knob, nearly at the midpoint of the planned road. Construction continued in segments. World War II and lack of federal funding delayed progress, so the project took more than half a century—construction was not complete until September 11, 1987, exactly fifty-two years later, when the last 6.5 miles were built in North Carolina. This stretch included the architecturally impressive Linn Cove Viaduct, a soaring bridge that carefully lifts the Parkway up and around the fragile ecosystems of Grandfather Mountain, protected by its owner, naturalist Hugh Morton.

The sun sinks downward in the late afternoon over Graveyard Fields, a popular hiking spot at the edge of Haywood County, North Carolina. Sometime in the distant past a windstorm broke the spruce trees that grew here, and grasses grew over them, creating shapes that looked like graves. A fire in 1925 contributed further to this spare landscape.

The end result is an incredible construction, a corridor of trees, mountains and roads, where human endeavor and the natural world meet and coexist. Stanley Abbott called it "the brush of a comet's tail." Parkway historian Harley Jolley more recently has likened it to "a grand balcony." The Blue Ridge Parkway is a road like no other, a road that cuts a cross-section through natural ecosystems and man-made communities alike, its brilliant design curving around the highest points of the mountains.

In a time when highways have become the speed of life, from the dangerous and polluted interstates to the instantaneous communications through cyberspace's information highways, the Blue Ridge Parkway is a different kind of journey. It's a welcome step back in time and place, a retreat to a purer world, a path through parts of the world that have been here for time untold and will still exist when we have gone.

The Appalachian Mountains date back 230 million years, and the rock that is at their roots formed 500 million to 1 billion years ago under long-gone oceans. Humans were here no more than 8,000 years ago, from what we can learn from archaeological evidence left behind. The mountains are shifting slowly upward—one and a half inches every 1,000 years.

Even the Parkway's physical shape makes it impossible to rush through. The speed limit is 45 miles per hour from beginning to end; overlooks curve away from the road and invite motorists to stop and sit a while; there are no advertisements or highway signs to distract travelers from the beauty of the Parkway experience.

The Parkway begins in the Great Valley of Virginia, the Shenandoah. Its name meant "Daughter of the Stars" to the Native Americans who first dwelled here. Fertile and wide, the valley was nicknamed the "Breadbasket of the South," and agriculture is still important here today. Farms and grazing cattle dot the countryside. It was the site of Civil War battles and the golden age of the railroads, and underground, caverns lace the earth.

This area was settled by Scotch-Irish and German pioneers. It's Thomas Jefferson's home country, where he built Monticello and Poplar Forest and for a time owned Natural Bridge, which George Washington surveyed. Transportation history laces the valley—canals along the James River (first suggested by George Washington) were major trade routes before the railroads came. Photographer O. Winston Link documented much the demise of the railroad throughout this region, photographing the last of the steam engines.

The mountains grow gradually taller as the road moves south, traveling out of the Shenandoah Valley and into the Roanoke Valley, climbing into the southern plateaus. Roanoke, population 100,000, is one of the two largest cities along the Parkway—the other, to the south, is Asheville, North Carolina. Both have thriving arts communities and historic downtowns, and both have succeeded in blending history and progress, cityscape and landscape.

The North Carolina end of the Parkway is tall and craggy; this is waterfall country, too. Here the Blue Ridge gives way to the Black Mountains and the Great Craggy and Great Balsam mountain ranges before the Parkway curves into the grandeur of the Great Smoky Mountains. The slopes are steeper here— some of the highest peaks in the eastern United States—and 6,684-foot Mt. Mitchell tops them all. From this mountain's top you can see for 70 miles on a clear day. Around Haywood and Jackson counties are the highest and most isolated miles of the Parkway, the site of Richland Balsam Knob (the Parkway's highest point), Graveyard Fields and Shining Rock Wilderness.

"Preserve" is an important word in the life of the Blue Ridge Parkway. From the beginning, it was built so that its past would be kept intact, from restoring historic mills and cabins along the way to creating visitor centers and museums. On Grandfather

Brilliant azaleas bloom around a tree trunk in the Ravens Roost area, around milepost 10.7. Wildflowers grow in profusion all along the Parkway. Two centuries ago, naturalist John Bartram discovered and nearly kept secret the treasure of wildflowers in the Shenandoah Valley.

Mountain, 21 species of salamanders (three were discovered here), more than 20 species of warblers, and rare creatures such as the saw-whet owl and peregrine falcon have been protected.

The Parkway's biological range is as broad as its geological one. The drastic differences in elevation create habitats that are

Love Gap, just 15 miles from the northern terminus of the Parkway, was named for the community that was once here, which was said to be named after the daughter of its first postmaster. Until the post office closed in 1944, Love, Virginia was a pausing point for countless love letters that were sent here for a sentimental postmark on February 14.

diverse with plant and animal life, and the highest elevations more closely match the Canadian tundra than the American south. Rainfall, wind and forest fires create and re-create the environments along the Parkway. Early naturalists including William Bartram, Andre Michaux, John Fraser and Asa Gray explored these mountains, and their names remain with the species they discovered, including Gray's lily and Lyon's turtlehead. More than 300 flowering plants are estimated to live in the Parkway corridor.

There's wildlife, too, from chattering squirrels to an occasional black bear. White-tailed deer, while commonly seen now along the roadsides and in the parks, were nearly hunted out of existence. They were successfully reintroduced to this region in the 1900s. More recently, elk, which disappeared years ago from the mountains, have been reintroduced in the Cataloochee Valley area of North Carolina. Other species, like the colossal chestnut trees destroyed by logging and insects, are lost to history.

But history—human and natural—is clearly visible along the Blue Ridge Parkway, which could be considered a long living-history museum. Groups such as the Southern Highland Craft Guild have kept cultural history alive at Asheville's Folk Art Center. Organizations such as FRIENDS of the Blue Ridge Parkway and the Western Virginia Land Trust work to ensure that scenic views don't disappear under commercial development.

In 2000, the Blue Ridge Music Center opened at Fisher's Peak near Galax, a center of Appalachian musicmaking, at Virginia milepost 213. In the summer, local, regional and national musicians perform weekly, and people can visit the luthier's shop and visitor center or hike on the trails.

Stops along the Parkway combine history with recreation. Peaks of Otter, at milepost 86, has a lakeside lodge, hiking trails to 360-degree views, a restored historic farm and the oldest tavern in the region preserved on its property. Virginia's Explore Park, at milepost 115, has preserved and restored historic buildings, including a gristmill and church, and celebrates mountain culture in festivals, art exhibits, historical demonstrations and music. Mabry Mill (milepost 176.2), possibly the most photographed site on the Parkway, is still grinding grain after all these years, and features live music and apple butter-making.

If Virginia is the musical end of the Parkway, North Carolina is the visual; communities throughout the western region continue their tradition of art and craft. Moses Cone Manor near Asheville was once a summer mansion; today, visitors can hike, ride horses or cross-country ski along its carriage roads, and there's a craft shop there, too. Little Switzerland, at milepost 329, is a restored apple orchard first planted by the Clinchfield Railroad, today the site of live music and craft demonstrations. Cherokee, at the very end of the Parkway, remembers Native American culture in museums and festivals.

Along the way, travelers can stop at campgrounds, lodges, lakes and restaurants, all part of the Parkway property. More than 350 miles of trails wind around and across the Blue Ridge Parkway, including portions of the Appalachian Trail and the North Carolina Mountains-to-Sea Trail. Vineyards, bed and breakfasts and historic communities are all within reach of this remarkable road.

The Blue Ridge Parkway is a journey through time as well as geography, climbing the highest peaks of the Appalachians and dipping into the rural countryside. It's a record of history, from the prehistoric to the Industrial Age, from Cherokee tribes to European immigrants. Teeming with life and overseeing the most beautiful vistas in the East, it carries us into the twenty-first century by preserving the centuries that have come before. The images in this book capture it in all its seasons, from the wildflowers of spring to the quiet of winter, with high summer and brilliant autumn in between. Enjoy your journey down this historic and beloved road.

A hiker pauses in a tunnel of rhododendron along the Appalachian Trail near Onion Mountain at milepost 79.7. Locals know Onion as Injin Mountain—Injin is the name for the wild onion (leek) that grows in these parts. Some call it the ramp, and festivals and ramp dinners celebrate the mountain edible every year.

RIGHT: The steep slopes of the mountains made farming difficult for early settlers. It's said that farmers used Twenty Minute Cliff, at milepost 19, to tell when the sun was going to set—they had 20 minutes left to plant corn when the light hit the cliffs.

FACING PAGE: Mountains slope gradually at the edges of Virginia's Shenandoah Valley. The land is wide here between the mountain ridges. The name Shenandoah, like the valley, echoes with Native American legend; translated, it means "Daughter of the Stars."

Sunrises can be fiery red over the mountaintops along the Parkway. This view is in the Green Knob area, near Moses H. Cone Memorial Park in North Carolina.

RIGHT: Rockfish Valley lies at the northern terminus of the Blue Ridge Parkway, where the valley is wide and the mountains rolling. The Tuscarora Indians settled here in the 1700s after they were driven from the Carolina coastlands.

BELOW: Sunset glows on bare trees high in the Black Mountains of North Carolina. Sturdy evergreens and rough shrubs thrive in the cold and wind of these high elevations.

LEFT: The Cherokee who once lived here believed that the stark stone face of Devil's Courthouse (North Carolina, milepost 422.4) hid a dwelling of the giant Judaculla, who danced there and entertained guests. A nature trail ascends the Courthouse, with a summit view of three river valleys.

BELOW: A split rail fence is a reminder of the older architecture of this area, when Parkway land was farmland where mountain settlers grew corn and raised cattle. This cabin, at Smart View (milepost 154.5), was the home of the Trail family in the 1890s. A picnic area and hiking trails are here now.

FACING PAGE: Wildflowers crowd a meadow at Volunteer Gap, said to be named for area residents who volunteered to build a road over the gap to Hillsville, Virginia in the 1800s.

BELOW: Gold drawn to gold, a yellow swallowtail lights on an equally yellow sunflower. Sunflowers grow in moist areas, and six species of them can be found along the Blue Ridge Parkway and its adjoining two parks, Great Smoky Mountains National Park and Shenandoah National Park.

LEFT: Bright red foliage and fair-weather cirrus clouds belie the name of this often-desolate spot, Graveyard Fields. Its landscape, laid bare by wind and fire, is slowly being reclaimed by trees and shrubs that are creeping back across the bald.

FACING PAGE: The Tanawha Trail stretches 13.5 miles from Julian Price Memorial Park to the Beacon's Height overlook, climbing the southeast side of Grandfather Mountain. This is a view from the trail on Rough Ridge, a mountain bald, with the Parkway visible in the distance.

FACING PAGE: The 3,900 acres of Julian Price Memorial Park stretch between milepost 295.5 and 300 in North Carolina. The lake, which reflects the colors of autumn from its wooded shoreline, is stocked with trout for fishing.

RIGHT: The forest floor is as rich as its grander upper stories, populated by mushrooms, mosses, ferns and wildflowers. Fungi help break down organic materials, which enriches the soil, and aid more complex plants in absorbing nutrients.

BELOW: The waters of the Linville River cut through granite and quartzite rock, creating Linville Falls at milepost 316.3.

FACING PAGE: The colors of the trees follow the changing of seasons, ever-higher ridges of forest turning from green to yellow to crimson as summer passes into autumn.

BELOW: High altitude and rainfall make Craggy Gardens, at milepost 364.5, an environment reminiscent of sub-arctic tundra. Flame azalea grows on this mountain bald, one of those mysterious bare summits that lost its trees in time forgotten, to grazing, ice, farming or insects—no one knows for sure.

FACING PAGE: A spill of red leaves carpets the ground under a solitary tree that is fading into fall. Wildflowers and late summer grasses crowd the banks of Little Glade Mill Pond at Cumberland Knob, just south of the North Carolina/Virginia line.

BELOW: White-tailed deer like this doe and fawn are graceful, common inhabitants of the Blue Ridge Parkway corridor. They almost disappeared from the Blue Ridge region, hunted, logged and farmed out of their habitats by the end of the nineteenth century. During the twentieth century, white-tailed deer were reintroduced to the park successfully; similar efforts are underway with elk and other species.

ABOVE: Every spring the dogwoods fill the mountains with white and pink swaths of blossoms. Christian legend has it that the dogwood was the tree that gave wood for Christ's cross; afterwards the tree, once tall and straight, was made short and curving so that it could never again be used for such a task. The notches in its four petals are said to represent Christ's wounds.

LEFT: Rocking chairs and a porch with a view—two important parts of southern mountain living. These rockers look out over the mountains from Mt. Pisgah Lodge, which is open April through October at milepost 408.6.

FACING PAGE: Sky and mountain meet above the Tye River Valley at the northern end of the Parkway.

RIGHT: The Linn Cove Viaduct was completed in 1987, the very last piece of the Blue Ridge Parkway to finish construction. Its architecture was the result of lobbying by Hugh Morton, owner of Grandfather Mountain, to preserve the mountainside it curves around.

BELOW: Also called "orange-plume," the yellow fringe orchid *(Habenaria ciliaris)* grows in low and middle altitudes along the Parkway, peaking in midsummer in meadows and open woods.

LEFT: The sunrise sparkles across the snow on the far side of Abbott Lake. A guest at Peaks of Otter lodge has left these footprints from an early morning walk in the quiet of winter.

FACING PAGE: Relics of the past lie quiet against the winter snow. Pictured is the Johnson Farm at Peaks of Otter, Virginia at milepost 86. Now the site of a winery, lodge and lake, Peaks of Otter were once hunting and camping grounds for the Cherokee. Restored on the property is Polly Woods' Ordinary, an inn from 1834 to 1860.

FAR RIGHT: The forest surrounding Brevard, North Carolina in Transylvania County is known for its waterfalls. One of the less grand but more interactive is Sliding Rock, which lets loose 11,000 gallons a minute over a 60-foot rock drop. Jeans hold up better than bathing suits here.

RIGHT: Pisgah National Forest near the Biltmore Estate is the home of the Cradle of Forestry in America—6,500 acres dedicated to the history of these woods and their upkeep, all the way back to the forest managers George Vanderbilt hired in the late-1800s (Gifford Pinchot and Carl A. Schenck). Pictured is Cantress Creek Lodge; there are historic cabins, a 1915 logging locomotive and a sawmill here, plus festivals, naturalist programs and concerts.

RIGHT: Fire pink *(Silene virginica)* flowers through the spring, and into summer in higher elevations. In the same family as the carnation and sometimes called the "catch-fly," it's found in open woods, hillsides and on rocky cliffs and banks.

BELOW: Rhododendron thrives in Craggy Gardens, around milepost 368. The North Carolina Mountains-to-Sea Trail crosses the mountain bald here, passing among sturdy vegetation that can survive the cold winter temperatures. Trees such as red oak, yellow birch and beech are bent by the wind and ice until they resemble old orchards.

LEFT: Spring blooms brilliant near the James River in Virginia; the James River overlook at milepost 63.6 is the lowest point on the Blue Ridge Parkway.

ABOVE: The sun disappears behind the mountains, leaving Craggy Gardens dim at dusk. Like many mountain balds, its mysterious clear expanse is disappearing under trees that are reclaiming the land.

RIGHT: Before the building of the railroads, the James River was the major commercial route from eastern Virginia into the Shenandoah Valley—double dugout canoes, pole-guided batteaux and tow barges ferried products from tobacco to plaster to pig iron through the ninety locks along its route. Today, an annual batteau festival commemorates this old trade.

LEFT: The cascades in E. B. Jeffress Park rush through the yellows and greens of the forest. Jeffress Park is the site of the Cascades Nature Trail; in the vicinity are Cool Spring Baptist Church and the Jesse Brown Cabin, remnants of families who lived here and ministers who preached here in the 1800s.

FACING PAGE: Leaves still cling stubbornly to autumn branches at Chestoa View, a rock balcony overlook reached by a short trail down Humpback Mountain at milepost 320.8. From the overlook, hikers can see Hawksbill, Grandfather, Linville and Tablerock mountains. Linville Gorge is below.

ABOVE: Mountain laurel *(Kalmia latifolia)* is one of the best-loved harbingers of summer. It blooms from May to July in the mountains, growing up to 10 feet high in rocky, wooded areas, filling the forest with splashes of white and pink.

FACING PAGE: The elegant drop of Crabtree Falls in Virginia (there is also a Crabtree Falls in North Carolina, around milepost 339.5) is a five- to six-mile drive from Parkway milepost 27.2, Tye River Gap. A 2.9-mile hike parallels Crabtree Creek through this lush green part of Nelson County.

ABOVE: Falling Water Cascades drops 200 feet in the Virginia woods at milepost 83.1. The waterfall is along a National Recreation Trail, and there are stone steps and a footbridge for visitors to follow.

LEFT: A hiker walks through a corridor of mountain laurel at Indian Gap, around milepost 47.5 in Virginia.

FACING PAGE: The land that is now occupied by the Humpback Rocks farmstead was once the William J. Carter Farm, though its original buildings have disappeared since the Carters lived here in the 1800s. Buildings from the same time period have been moved here for tours and historic interpretation, and the dogwood still blooms around them as it did more than a century ago.

Three aspects of history merge into one view near Galax, Virginia. Rough wooden rail fences border the road—fences (often made of chestnut) that used to crisscross this land when it was farms and pasture. In the 1930s the Blue Ridge Parkway came into being, a 469-mile length of carefully designed pavement and stone structures. Over it all arches the natural beauty that's been here since before history: the trees, the slopes, the skies.

RIGHT: The waterwheel still turns at Mabry Mill, one of the most-photographed spots on the Parkway (milepost 176.2), built in 1910 by E. B. Mabry, who operated it until the mid-1930s. Blacksmiths, a miller and mountain musicians liven up the scene here during warm weather, and fall at the mill means it's time to make apple butter.

BELOW: Rain beads on pink rhododendron, that other high-elevation flower that's often confused with mountain laurel. Rhododendron blooms pink, blue, purple and white depending on the species, and reaches its peak in June.

LEFT: The sun is gold on Flat Top Manor, a stately mansion at Moses H. Cone Memorial Park near Blowing Rock, North Carolina once owned by Moses Cone, who made his fortune in textile mills. A craft center, the remnants of apple orchards and two artificial lakes are still on the property. Twenty-five miles of carriage roads offer hiking, horseback riding and cross-country skiing.

BELOW: Fall leaves frame the mountains in the Buena Vista area of Rockbridge County, Virginia. The county is famous for its Civil War history (Lexington is the final resting place of two Confederate generals, Jackson and Lee) and for Natural Bridge, a stone arch Thomas Jefferson once owned. Another north-south road, U.S. 11, passes directly over the 215-foot-high span.

FACING PAGE: Caroline Brinegar, a weaver, lived in Brinegar Cabin between 1877 and 1935 after moving to the area from North Carolina. Family descendants still gather here for reunions.

BELOW: The Twin Tunnels, at milepost 344.5 and 344.7 in North Carolina, accomplish what the Parkway's designers set out to do—create a road that looked as if it grew out of the mountains themselves. These two tunnels look like caves in the rock. The northern tunnel measures 240 feet; the southern is 401 feet.

Deep purples and pinks of dawn blend into one
another as the moon sets over Price Lake, in Julian
Price Memorial Park, and mist rises from the still
surface of the water. The park's 3,900 acres
are slowly reverting to wilderness.

RIGHT: Fall shadows stretch across a curve in the road near Petites Gap, Milepost 70, near the James River in Virginia.

BELOW: Early in the twentieth century, logging companies built narrow-gauge railroads in the Blue Ridge Mountains. This section, reconstructed at Yankee Horse Ridge, is all that remains of a logging railroad that measured more than 50 miles and carried more than 100 million board feet of logs to a mill.

LEFT: The sky is purple mist at dusk, seen from the Chimney Rock overlook north of Route 60 in Virginia.

BELOW: Sunset at the Cowee overlook fades gold to violet, as beautiful as its Cherokee name.

RIGHT: Two great mountain ranges meet at Waterrock Knob: the Plott Balsam and the Great Balsam. At milepost 451.2, Waterrock Knob is the second highest altitude on the Blue Ridge Parkway. Nearby Waterrock Knob Trail is the highest trail on the Parkway, at an elevation of 6,400 feet.

FACING PAGE: A stairway of green climbs the Greenstone Trail at milepost 8.8. This area was once volcanically active, and there are still traces of lava flows nearby, as well as remnants of more recent stone phenomena: "hog walls" that plantation slaves built in the 1800s to corral wandering pigs.

RIGHT: Rock climbers hoist themselves up onto the rock face at Ravens Roost (milepost 10.7 in Virginia), which is popular with hang gliders (and with ravens). Cold weather and wind have cut into rock and trees here.

BELOW: Roanoke, Virginia lies along a rolling stretch of the Parkway, in a region historically agricultural. Forests interchange with pasture, and rail fences zigzag along many segments of road in this high country that marks the start of the Blue Ridge plateau.

RIGHT: Fog rolls in over the face of Grandfather Mountain in early fall. Grandfather's "old man" profile is not all there is—the mountain stretches 10 miles long and 3 miles wide, with elevations from 2,500 to 6,000 feet. Its wide range of habitats support a wide range of species, including rare saw-whet owls and more recorded salamander species than any other site in the United States.

BELOW: The Tanawha Trail crosses Rough Ridge, a heath bald at milepost 302.8 in North Carolina. Visible from the rocks is Grandfather Mountain and the curve of the Linn Cove Viaduct; along the trail is vegetation that includes rare lichens and other plants that thrive in the rough terrain.

LEFT: Wildflowers, bird box, grazing cow, and rail fence all create a rural picture along the Parkway near Cumberland Knob, where construction on the Parkway first began. Dr. Thomas Walker explored this area just below the North Carolina/Virginia line in the 1750s, naming the nearby summit after the Duke of Cumberland.

BELOW: The mountains of western North Carolina sparkle underground with gems— tourmaline, moonstone, opal and world-record sapphires are mined here. Even diamonds were occasionally found in the rocks here a century ago or more. The Museum of North Carolina Minerals, near Little Switzerland, features geology exhibits and a bookshop.

ABOVE: Trees frame a massive view in North Carolina's Black Balsam area. Forest fires and logging turned Black Balsam Knob into grass and scrub bald; serviceberry, yellow birch and mountain ash are now beginning to grow back where blackberries, blueberries and rhododendron had taken over.

FACING PAGE: A vast distance of valley opens up through a gap in Humpback Rocks, along the Appalachian Trail. The AT's 2,100-plus miles stretch from Georgia to Maine; Virginia's 540 miles of AT parallel the Blue Ridge Parkway, and North Carolina and Tennessee lay claim to another 288 miles.

ABOVE: Farmland is green and rolling near Whetstone Ridge (milepost 29), believed to be named after the sandstone found there, good for sharpening knives.

RIGHT: The Parkway passes through the arch of a tunnel near Sylva, North Carolina, the county seat of Jackson. There are twenty-six tunnels along the Parkway; the shortest (Rough Ridge Tunnel, milepost 349) is 150 feet long, and the longest (Pine Mountain Tunnel, milepost 399.1) stretches 1,434 feet.

ABOVE: A Canada lily *(Lilium canadense)* seems to peer downward. These delicately curving flowers grow in moist areas and low thickets, blooming in June and July. Their colors range from orange to red and purple.

LEFT: Cardinal flowers *(Lobelia cardinalis)* are in the bluebell family. They bloom July through September in wet areas—marshes and beside streams—and grow up to six feet in height.

FACING PAGE: Bluff Mountain Tunnel is half-hidden by brilliant crimson leaves. It's the only Parkway tunnel in Virginia, stretching 630 feet (milepost 53.1). Bluff Mountain overlook is just north at milepost 52.8. Legend has it that Bluff Mountain is haunted by the ghost of four-year-old Ottie Cline Powell, who was lost in 1890 when he went looking for firewood.

Roanoke, Virginia is one of the two largest cities along the Blue Ridge Parkway (the other is Asheville, North Carolina). It's called "Star City of the South," and the overlook at Mill Mountain embraces a view of the city circled by mountains. Not visible here is the reason for Roanoke's nickname: a half-century-old neon-lit star that shines for miles year-round.

Mount Mitchell is the final resting place of the explorer who lost his life measuring it. Elisha Mitchell proved that his namesake peak was in fact taller than Grandfather Mountain, believed at the time to be the tallest mountain in the East. Mitchell died during an 1857 trek and is buried at the base of the tower. Mount Mitchell became North Carolina's first state park in 1915.

LEFT: Sharp Top, one of the Peaks of Otter in Virginia's Bedford County, overlooks Abbott Lake and the Blue Ridge mountains fading into the distance.

BELOW: Dogwood blossoms, the familiar beauty of mountain springs, frames the lodge at Peaks of Otter, a favorite retreat at milepost 86.

Pat and Chuck Blackley are a photographic and writing team who work throughout North America. With a love of the outdoors and of the Blue Ridge Mountains in particular, they find the Blue Ridge Parkway to be a favorite subject.

Their work appears in numerous magazines including *Backpacker, Blue Ridge Country, Country, Family Fun, Outdoor America,* and *Travel Holiday,* and in books by such publishers as Falcon, Farcountry Press, IDG Books (Frommer's), Insight Guides, Leisure Publishing, Lerner, National Geographic, Ulysses Press, and Walking Stick Press. Additionally, American Park Network, Forbes Special Interest, Impact Photographics, KC Publications, Virginia Tourism Corporation, and The Wilderness Society publish the Blackleys in calendars and commercial projects.

Writer and editor **Cara Ellen Modisett** has lived her life in the Shenandoah Valley. Her family's roots are in Page County, Virginia; she grew up in Harrisonburg, has lived the last five years in Roanoke and travels extensively throughout the Blue Ridge region as a writer and radio reporter.

Cara graduated *summa cum laude* from James Madison University in piano performance and English education. Since 1998 she has been on the staff of Leisure Publishing and serves as associate editor and project writer for many of Leisure's publications, including *Blue Ridge Country* and *The Roanoker* magazines. Cara has written for *American Forests* and *Virginia Living;* she co-produces a weekly arts show on WVTF Virginia public radio and edits *High Vistas,* the newsletter for FRIENDS of the Blue Ridge Parkway.